THIS TREE
WILL BE HERE
FOR A
THOUSAND YEARS

Other books by Robert Bly

Poetry

SILENCE IN THE SNOWY FIELDS

THE LIGHT AROUND THE BODY

THE TEETH MOTHER NAKED AT LAST

JUMPING OUT OF BED

SLEEPERS JOINING HANDS

OLD MAN RUBBING HIS EYES

THE MORNING GLORY

THIS BODY IS MADE OF CAMPHOR AND GOPHERWOOD

Translations (poetry)

TWENTY POEMS OF GEORG TRAKL (WITH JAMES WRIGHT)

NERUDA AND VALLEJO: SELECTED POEMS (WITH JAMES WRIGHT
AND JOHN KNOEPFLE)

LORCA AND JIMENEZ: SELECTED POEMS

FRIENDS, YOU DRANK SOME DARKNESS. MARTINSON, EKELOF
AND TRANSTROMER: SELECTED POEMS

RILKE: TEN SONNETS TO ORPHEUS

THE KABIR BOOK: 44 OF THE ECSTATIC POEMS OF KABIR

Translations (fiction)

HUNGER, BY KNUT HAMSUN

THE STORY OF GOSTA BERLING, BY SELMA LAGERLÖF

Interviews

TALKING ALL MORNING: COLLECTED INTERVIEWS AND
CONVERSATIONS

THIS TREE
WILL BE HERE
FOR A
THOUSAND YEARS

ROBERT BLY

HARPER & ROW, PUBLISHERS
New York, Hagerstown, San Francisco, London

Grateful acknowledgment is made to the editors of the following magazines in which some of these poems were first printed: STONE DRUM, KAMADHENU, SUENOS, CHELSEA, THIN LINE, POET AND CRITIC, TENNESSEE POETRY JOURNAL, OHIO REVIEW, FIELD, U T REVIEW, CRAZY HORSE, MODERN OCCASIONS, KAYAK, WESTIGAN REVIEW, VANDERBILT POETRY REVIEW, ALTERNATIVE PRESS BROADSIDE SERIES, THE GEORGIA REVIEW, PLAINSONG, THE TOWER, RAPPORT, NEW LETTERS, THE SMALL FARM, NEW SALT CREEK READER, THE NORTH STONE REVIEW, PARTISAN REVIEW, PERIPHERY, PEACE AND PIECES, and DAKOTAH TERRITORY. "A Dream in November" was the original title of "A Dream on the Night of First Snow" when it first appeared in POETRY (CHICAGO).

FIRST EDITION

Designed by Janice Stern

Library of Congress Cataloging in Publication Data

Bly, Robert.
  This tree will be here for a thousand years.
    I. Title.
PS3552.L9T55   811'.5'4   78-22449
ISBN 0-06-010358-2
ISBN 0-06-090713-4 pbk.

79 80 81 82 83 10 9 8 7 6 5 4 3 2 1

For Biddy
who came to meet me

Contents

6

II

The Two Presences

More and more I notice a sort of ground tone audible under the words of poems. The ground tone in these poems is the consciousness *out there* among plants and animals. One day sitting depressed in a cabin on the shore of a small lake, I wrote about the depression:

> Mist: no one on the other shore.
> It may be that these trees
> I see have consciousness,
> and this desire to weep comes from them.

Many people who think about it believe that the desire to weep comes entirely from inside us. Conservatives in these matters declare that human intelligence stands alone facing a world that appears sometimes hostile, sometimes inviting, but that actually possesses neither intelligence nor consciousness. Many ancient Greek poems, on the other hand, suggest that human beings and the "green world" share a consciousness. Each of the poems that follow contains an instant, sometimes twenty seconds long, sometimes longer, when I was aware of two separate energies: my own consciousness, which is insecure, anxious, massive, earthbound, persistent, cunning, hopeful; and a second consciousness which is none of these things. The second consciousness has a melancholy tone, the tear inside the stone, what Lucretius calls "the tears of

9

things", an energy circling downward, felt often in autumn, or moving slowly around apple trees or stars.

In a few poems what is inside and what is outside merge, so that even the writer cannot tell which is which. That is lucky, but doesn't happen often. Being divided myself, I rarely achieve a poem where the inner and outer merge without a seam. So I am describing what my artistic intentions are, rather than what I have achieved.

I've come to believe, however, that it is important for everyone that the second consciousness appear somehow in the poem, merged or not. It's time. The "human" poem can become transparent or porous at the end, so that the city, or objects, or the countryside enters. Antonio Machado's poems sometimes open out that way. It's helpful if you're writing about a pine to go to the pine, or about a tunnel to go to the tunnel, and I've noticed how difficult it is to write poems in this genre at a desk.

When the writer tries for a union of inner and outer in the same poem, he can fail in several distinct ways. A "descriptive poem" is a failure, for it includes only the object, perhaps many details of it, but without its inner grief. Or it can have that, but the psychic container of the writer is missing. I've thrown away many such poems. I have also failed at times in the other way—times in which I sensed very well what was going on in my own psyche, and I allowed words to come in and soak that up, but I was too asleep to let the other water in.

Among poems I have kept, I have spent dozens of hours on quite slender poems—"Amazed by an Accumulation of Snow" is one example; and the hard thing for me is to find a sequence of sounds, a rhythm, and an image that carries the inner and outer together without letting either fall.

So sometimes I admire the poems that follow for their quality of doubleness, of the complicated consciousness, the presence in them simultaneously of two presences. The mood is impersonal, as in all works of art that are interested in some consciousness beside the author's. Sometimes they seem to me too impersonal.

These poems then form a volume added to *Silence in the Snowy Fields;* the two books make one book. Like the earlier poems, these poems try to achieve "two presences" by adopting the line with simple syntax, and the book includes the poems I have written in this style since *Silence in the Snowy Fields* was published in 1962.

After a storm the leafy tree is no longer solid,
but the pine still throws a full shadow.
It has found a place to be.
For a thousand years it will not give up this place.

—TAO YUAN-MING

I

October Frost

Last night the first heavy frost.
Now the brave alfalfa has sobered.
It has folded, as if from great heat,
and turned away from the north.
The horse's winter coat has come
through the bark of the trees.
Our ears hear tinier sounds,
reaching far away east in the early darkness.

Writing Again

Oval
faces crowding to the window!
I turn away,
disturbed—

When I write of moral things,
the clouds boil
blackly!
By day's end
a room of restless people,
lifting and putting down small things.

Well that is how I have spent this day.
And what good will it do me in the grave?

Fall Poem

There are eyes in the dry wisps of grass,
and invisible claws in the rooster's eyes,
the patient feet of old men in the boards left
    out all summer.

Something is about to happen!
Christ will return!
But each fall it goes by without happening.

The end of the pickup disappears down the road,
the pigweed bent over like abandoned machines . . .

Sitting in Fall Grass

All day wind had called me,
oceans, a yellow line streaking
across the sky,
bones thrown out.

I walked to my sitting place,
I sat down.

As we close our eyes, what
piles of bones we see!
Ruined castles,
trampled cinnamon,
crinoline crushed in long grass.

And voices that say,
I am not like you . . .
I must live so . . . condemned
by an old yellow lion . . .

Night Farmyard

The horse lay on his knees sleeping.
A rat hopped across scattered hay
and disappeared under the henhouse.
There the chickens sat in a stiff darkness.

Asleep they are bark fallen from an old cottonwood.
Yet we know their soul is gone, risen
far into the upper air about the moon.

Dawn in Threshing Time

The three-bottom plow is standing in the corner of a stubble field. The flax straw lies exhausted on the ground.

The dawning sun slants over the wet pigeon grass, so that the slope of highway ditches is like a face awakening from sleep.

The oat stubble is shiny. The farmer puts on his jacket and goes out. Swaths still to be combined are wet. Every morning as he gets up after thirty he puts on besides his jacket the knowledge that he is not strong enough to die, which he first felt deep in his wooden cradle at threshing time.

Reading in Fall Rain

The fields are black once more.
The old restlessness is going.
I reach out with open arms
to pull in the black fields.

All morning rain has fallen
steadily on the roof.
I feel like a butterfly
joyful in its powerful cocoon.

*

I break off reading:
one of my bodies is gone!
It's outdoors, walking
swiftly away in the rain!

I get up and look out.
Sure enough, I see
the rooster lifting his legs
high in the wet grass.

Insect Heads

Those insects, golden
and Arabic, sailing in the husks of galleons,
their octagonal heads also
hold sand paintings of the next life.

To Live

"Living" means eating up particles of death,
    as a child picks up crumbs from around the table.
"Floating" means letting the crumbs fall behind you on
    the path.
To live is to rush ahead eating up your own death,
    like an endgate, open, hurrying into night.

Cornpicker Poem

1

Sheds left out in the darkness,
abandoned granaries, cats merging into the night.

There are hubcaps cooling in a dark yard.

The stiff-haired son has slouched in
and gone to bed.
A low wind sweeps over the moony land.

2

Overshoes stiffen in the entry.
The calendar grows rigid on the wall.

He dreams, and his body grows limber.
He is fighting a many-armed woman,
he is a struggler, he will not yield.
He fights her in the crotch of a willow tree.

He wakes up with jaws set,
and a victory.

3

It is dawn. Cornpicking today.
He leans over, hurtling
his old Pontiac down the road.

Somewhere the sullen chilled machine
is waiting, its empty gas cans around it.

Prophets

There are fields of white roses
with prophets asleep in them—
I see their long black feet.

Listening to a Cricket in the Wainscoting

That sound of his is like a boat with black sails.
Or a widow under a redwood tree, warning
passersby that the tree is about to fall.
Or a bell made of black tin in a Mexican village.
Or the hair in the ear of a hundred-year-old man!

Thinking of "Seclusion"

I get up late and ask what has to be done today.
Nothing has to be done, so the farm looks doubly good.
The blowing maple leaves fit so well with the moving
    grass.
The shadow of my writing shack looks small beside the
    growing trees.

Never be with your children, let them get stringy like
    radishes!
Let your wife worry about the lack of money!
Your whole life is like some drunkard's dream!
You haven't combed your hair for a whole month!

Digging Worms

Here I am, digging worms behind the chickenhouse,
the clods fall open when I hit
them with a tine, worms fall out . . .

Dreams press us on all sides, we stagger
along a wire, our children balance us
on their shoulders, we balance their graves
on ours.

Their graves are light. And we unwind
from some kind of cocoon made by lovers . . .
the old tires we used to swing on,
going faster, around and around, until

with one lurch we grow still and look down at our shoes.
Last night I dreamt my carelessness started stones
        dislodging near a castle. The stones
did not hurt my shoulders when they hit and went
        through,
but the wall of the castle fell.

Walking and Sitting

That's odd—I am trying to sit still,
trying to hold the mind to one thing.
Outdoors angleworms stretched out thin in the gravel,
while it is thundering.

A Long Walk Before the Snows Began

1

Nearly winter. All day the sky gray. Earth heavy.
The cornfields dead. I walk over the soaked
cornstalks knocked flat in rows,
a few grains of white sleet on the leaves.

2

White sleet also in the black plowing.
I turn and go west—tracks, pushed deep!
I am walking with an immense deer.
He passed three days ago.

3

I reach the creek at last, nearly dusk.
New snow on the river ice, under willow branches,
open places like the plains of North China,
where the mice have been, just a half hour ago.

4

It must be that I will die one day!
I see my body lying stretched out.
A woman whose face I cannot see stands near my body.
A column of smoke rises from Vonderharr's field.

A Dream on the Night of First Snow

I woke from a first-day-of-snow dream.
I met a girl in an attic,
    who talked of operas, intensely.
Snow has bent the poplar over nearly to the ground,
new snowfall widens the plowing.
Outside, maple leaves float on rainwater,
    yellow, matted, luminous.
I saw a salamander . . . I took him up . . .
he was cold. When I put him down again,
    he strode over a log
with such confidence, like a chessmaster,
    the front leg first, then the hind
    leg, he rose up like a tractor climbing
    over a hump in the field
and disappeared toward winter, a caravan going deeper
    into mountains,
dogs pulling travois,
feathers fluttering on the lances of the arrogant men.

A Walk

It is a pale tree,
all alone in January snow.
Beneath it a shoot
eaten pale by a rabbit . . .

Looking up I see the farmyards with their groves—
the pines somber,
made for winter, they knew it would come . . .

And the cows inside the barn, caring nothing for all this,
their noses in the incense hay,
half-drunk, dusk comes as it was promised
to them by *their* savior.

Roads

In memoriam

Last night, full moon.
The snowy fields, the roads silent and alone.
Clods rose above the snow in the plowing west,
like mountain tops, or the chest of graves.

Passing an Orchard by Train

Grass high under apple trees.
The bark of the trees rough and sexual,
the grass growing heavy and uneven.

We cannot bear disaster, like
the rocks—
swaying nakedly
in open fields.

One slight bruise and we die!
I know no one on this train.
A man comes walking down the aisle.
I want to tell him
that I forgive him, that I want him
to forgive me.

II

Women We Never See Again

There are women we love whom we never see again.
They are chestnuts shining in the rain.
Moths hatched in winter disappear behind books.
Sometimes when you put your hand into a hollow tree
you touch the dark places between the stars.
Human war has parted messengers from another planet,
who cross back to each other at night,
going through slippery valleys, farmyards where the rain
    has washed out all tracks,
and when we walk there, with no guide, saddened, in the
    dark
we see above us glowing the fortress made of ecstatic blue
    stone.

November Fog

This private misty day
with the lake so utterly cast down, like
a child
The long anxious wheels
churning in sand,
the pale willow leaves shedding light
around the "pale bride and groom."

Ant Heaps by the Path

I love to stare at old wooden doors after working,
the cough the ant family makes in ground,
the blackish stain around screwheads.

How much labor is needed to live our four lives!
Something turns its shoulders. When we do work
holes appear in the mountainside, no labor at all.

Amazed by an Accumulation of Snow

I had been singing alone in my darkened house
about a man who agrees to endure suffering.
The door opened, I was amazed to see the air thick;
the horse had turned his rump to the north.
Snow flows along the valleys of his back.
The white roof stood calmly among the black trees.

It is a shock that snow fell over the whole farm
while the singer remained private and alone in his house.
It is as if the African heron carved of buffalo horn
suddenly would open his mouth and call,
or a bell from under glass would lift and ring.
The horse's hoof kicks up a seashell, and the farmer
finds an Indian stone with a hole all the way through.

Pulling a Rowboat Up Among Lake Reeds

In the Ashby reeds it is already night,
though it is still day out on the lake.
Darkness has soaked into the shaded sand.
And how many other darknesses it reminds me of!
The darkness the moment after a child is born,
blood pouring from the animal's neck,
the slender metal climbing toward the moon.

Moving Books to a New Study

First snow yesterday, and now more falling.
Each blade has its own snow balanced on it.
One mousetrack in the snow ahead,
the tailmark wavering in
between the footprints. Dusk in half an hour.

Looking up I see my parents' grove.
Somehow neither the Norwegian culture
nor the American could keep them warm.
I walk around the barn the long way
carrying the heavy green book I love through the snow.

Driving My Parents Home at Christmas

As I drive my parents home through the snow,
their frailty hesitates on the edge of a mountainside.
I call over the cliff,
only snow answers.
They talk quietly
of hauling water, of eating an orange,
of a grandchild's photograph left behind last night.
When they open the door of their house, they disappear.
And the oak when it falls in the forest who hears it
        through miles and miles of silence?
They sit so close to each other . . . as if pressed together
        by the snow.

After a Day of Work

How lightly the legs walk over the snow-whitened fields!
I wander far off, like a daddy-longlegs blown over the
     water.
All day I worked alone, hour after hour.
It is January, easy walking, the big snows still to come.

Walking Where the Plows Have Been Turning

*"The most beautiful music of all is the music of
what happens."—old Irish tale*

for Joya Tempenelli

Some intensity of the body came to me at five in the morning.
I woke up, I saw the east pale with its excited brood. I slipped
from bed, and out the back door, onto the sleek and resigned
cottonwood leaves. The horses are out, eating in the ditch
. . . I walk down the road toward the west.

I notice a pebble on the road, then a corn-ear lying in the
ditchgrass, then an earthbridge into the cornfield. I walk on
it to the backland where the plows turn, the tractor tires have
married it, they love it more than the rest, cozy with bare dirt,
the downturned face of the plow that looked at it each
round . . .

In the risen sun the earth provides a cornhusk in one
place, a cottonwood tree in another, for no apparent reason.
A branch has dropped onto the fence wire, there are eternities
near, the body free of its exasperations, ready to see what will
happen. There is a humming in my body, it is jealous of no
one. The cricket lays its wings one over the other, a faint
whispery sound rises up to its head . . . which it hears . . . and
disregards . . . listening for the next sound . . .

July Morning

The day is awake. The bark calls to the rain still in the
    cloud.
"Never forget the lonely taste of the white dew."
And woolen robed drummers call on the naked to dance,
all the particles of the body shout together.

Sitting on the disc, the morning dove coos a porch,
    then a cathedral,
then the two arms of the cross!

He gives the nose, then the head, then the two ears
    of this rabbit
hopping along the garden,
then his death . . .

After that we will be alone in the deep blue reaches of the
    river.

An Empty Place

Empty places are white and light-footed. "Taking the road" means being willing to die, as the pigeon grass clump, that dies so quietly. There is a joy in emptiness. One day I saw an empty corncob on the ground, so beautiful, and where each kernel had been, there was a place to live.

The eyes are drawn to the dusty ground in fall—
small pieces of crushed oyster shell,
like doors into the earth made of mother-of-pearl;
slivers of glass,
a white chicken's feather that still seems excited by the
    warm blood,
and a corncob, all kernels gone, room after room in its
    endless palace . . .
this is the place of many mansions,
which Christ has gone to prepare for us.

Prayer Service in an English Church

Looking at the open page of the psalm book,
I see a ghostly knot floating in the paper!

Circles within circles on the page, floating,
showing that a branch once lived there!

Looking at the knot long and long,
I hear the priest call on the Saviour to come again.

The old around me keep on singing . . .
If the Saviour is a branch, how can he come again?

And the last day . . .
the whispers we will make from the darkening pillow . . .

Fishing on a Lake at Night

Someone has left a light on at the boathouse
to guide the fishermen back after dark.
The light makes no sound as it comes.
It flies over the waves like a bird with one wing.
Its path is a boatful of the dead, trying to return to life
over the broken waters.

And the light
simply comes, bearing no gifts,
as if the camels had arrived without the Wise Men.
It is steady, holding us to our old mountain home.
Now as we watch the moon rises over the popple forest.
It too arrives without fuss,
it goes between the boards around the pulp-cutter's house—
the same fence we pass through by opening the gate.

Night of First Snow

Night of first snow.
I stand, my back against a board fence.
The fir trees are black at the trunk, white out on the
    edges.
The earth balances all around my feet.

The apple trunk joins the white ground with what is
    above.
Fir branches balance the snow.
I too am a dark shape vertical to the earth.
All over the sky, the gray color that pleases the snow
    mother.

A woman wades out toward the wicker basket, floating,
rocking in darkening reeds.
The child and the light are half asleep.
What is human lies in the way the basket is rocking.

Black and white end in the gray color of the sky.
What is human lies in the three hairs, caught,
the rabbit left behind
as he scooted under the granary joist.

Solitude of the Two Day Snowstorm

Supper time . . . I open the door and go out . . . something blowing among the tree trunks . . . our own frail impulses go to shelter behind thin trees, or sail with the wind—

It is night . . . this is the time when after long hours alone, I sit with my family, and feel them near . . . at what I want to do I fail fifty times a day, and am confused . . . At last I go to bed.

At five I wake, strong wind around the north bedroom windows. I get up and go out, there is dust of snow on yesterday's ice. The snow grows gradually, the winds do not stop.

By afternoon, I lie listening to the wind . . . still going on . . . rising and wailing, sometimes with a sudden sweep, a woman's skirt pulled swiftly along the floor . . . at other times it gives a steady growl without anger, like the word "Enoch" . . . I stand up and look out.

The crow's head I found by the bridge this summer, and brought home, sits on the window sash, the one black thing before all that white. The head looks intense, swift, decided, the beak partly open, the eyes sunk. Among that soft white, the head looks like a warship . . . snow-blankets suddenly fall off the window screen behind him . . .

Frost Still in the Ground

I walk out in the fields; the frost is still in the ground.
It's like someone just beginning to write, and nothing has
    been said!

The shadows that come from another life
gather in folds around his head.

So I am, all at once. What I have
to say I have not said.

The snow water glances up at the new moon. It is
its own pond. In its lake the serpent is asleep.

Late Moon

The third week moon reaches its light over my father's
    farm,
half of it dark now, in the west that eats it away.
The earth has rocks in it that hum at early dawn.
As I turn to go in, I see my shadow reach for the latch.

A Dream of Retarded Children

That afternoon I had been fishing alone,
strong wind, some water slopping in the back of the boat.
I was far from home.
Later I woke several times hearing geese.
I dreamt I saw retarded children playing,
    and one came near.
And her teacher, the face open, hair light.
For the first time I forgot my distance,
I took her in my arms and held her.

Waking up, I felt how alone I was.
I walked on the dock.
Fishing alone in the far north.

Black Pony Eating Grass

Near me a black and shaggy pony is eating grass,
that crunching is night being ripped away from day,
a crystal's sound when it regains its twelve sides.

Our life is a house between two hills.
Flowers stand open on the altar,
the moonlight hugs the sides of popples.

In a few years we will die,
yet the grass continues to lift itself into the horse's teeth,
sharp harsh lines run through our bodies.
A star is also a stubborn man—
the Great Bear is seven old men walking.

The Fallen Tree

After a long walk I come down to the shore.
A cottonwood tree lies stretched out in the grass.
This tree knocked down by lightning—
and a hollow the owls made open now to the rain.
Disasters are all right, if they teach
    men and women
to turn their hollow places up.

The tree lies stretched out
    where it fell in the grass.
It is so mysterious, waters below, waters above,
so little of it we can ever know!

A Dream of an Afternoon with a
Woman I Did Not Know

I woke up, and went out. Not yet dawn.
A rooster claimed he was the sickle moon.
The windmill was a ladder that ended at a gray cloud.
A feed grinder was growling at a nearby farm.

Frost has made clouds of the weeds overnight.
In my dream we stopped for coffee, we sat alone
near a fireplace, near delicate cups.
I loved that afternoon, and the rest of my life.

Nailing a Dock Together

The dock is done, pulled out in the lake. How I love
putting my wet foot
on the boards I sawed myself!
It is a ladder stretching back to land . . .

So many secrets are still hidden.
A walker digs up a tin box with secrets
and then joyfully buries it again
so that the night and day will remain fresh.

The horse stands penned, but is also free.
It is a horse whose neck human
beings have longed to touch for centuries.
He stands in a stable of invisible wood.

An Evening When the Full Moon
Rose as the Sun Set

APRIL 11, 1976

The sun goes down in the dusty April night.
"You know it could be alive!"
The sun is round, massive, compelling, sober, on fire.
It moves swiftly through the tree-stalks of the Lundin
        grove as we drive past . . .
The legs of a bronze god walking at the edge of the world,
        unseen by many,
on his archaic errands, doubled up on his own energy.
He guides his life by his dreams,
when we look again he is gone.

Turning toward Milan, we see the other one, the moon,
        whole and rising.
Three wild geese make dark spots in that part of the sky.
Under the shining one the pastures leap forward,
grass fields rolling as in October, the sow-colored fields
        near the river.
This rising one lights the pair of pintails alert in the
        shallow pond.
It shines on those faithful to each other, alert in the early
        night.
And the life of faithfulness goes by like a river,
with no one noticing it.

Out Picking Up Corn

It is late December. I walk through the pasture,
Light on the hillocks, light
in the rolling mounds, eaten clean by horse teeth.

Then the black plowing, clods turned up,
the shoe looks for solid home.
A half covered ear of corn
not found by a deer.

I am learning; I walk through the plowed fields,
with a bag, picking up corn for the horses.
Some small pebbles on the dirt road
alight in the late sun.
Surely we do not eat only with our mouths,
or drink only by lifting our hands!

Who is this out gathering moss by the sea shore?
"My master has gone picking ferns on the mountain."
No one knows what they were picking,
what they drink is something respectable people do not
        want to take in,
walking in fog near the cliff.

P6